Books in the ABICS Publications Series

Badiru, Deji, **Youth Soccer Training Slides: A Math and Science Approach**, iUniverse, Bloomington, Indiana, USA, 2014

Badiru, Deji, **My Little Blue Book of Project Management: What, When, Who, and How**, iUniverse, Bloomington, Indiana, USA, 2014

Badiru, Deji, **8 by 3 Model of Time Management: Balancing Work, Home, and Leisure**, iUniverse, Bloomington, Indiana, USA, 2013

Badiru, Deji, **Badiru's Equation of Success: Intelligence, Common Sense, and Self-discipline**, iUniverse, Bloomington, Indiana, USA, 2013

Badiru, Deji, **Blessings of a Father: Education Contributions of Father Slattery at Saint Finbarr's College**, Bloomington, Indiana, USA, 2013

Badiru, Iswat and Deji Badiru, **Isi Cookbook: Collection of Easy Nigerian Recipes**,

iUniverse, Bloomington, Indiana, USA, 2013

Badiru, Deji and Iswat Badiru, **Physics in the Nigerian Kitchen: The Science, the Art, and the Recipes**, iUniverse, Bloomington, Indiana, USA, 2013.

Badiru, Deji, **Physics of Soccer: Using Math and Science to Improve Your Game**, iUniverse, Bloomington, Indiana, USA, 2010.

Badiru, Deji, **Getting things done through project management**, iUniverse, Bloomington, Indiana, USA, 2009.

ABICS Publications
A Division of
AB International Consulting Services (ABICS)
www.ABICSPublications.com
Books for home, work, and leisure

Youth Soccer Training Slides

A Math and Science Approach

Deji Badiru

iUniverse LLC
Bloomington

YOUTH SOCCER TRAINING SLIDES
A MATH AND SCIENCE APPROACH

iUniverse books may be ordered through booksellers or by contacting:

iUniverse LLC
1663 Liberty Drive
Bloomington, IN 47403
www.iuniverse.com
1-800-Authors (1-800-288-4677)

Because of the dynamic nature of the Internet, any web addresses or links contained in this book may have changed since publication and may no longer be valid. The views expressed in this work are solely those of the author and do not necessarily reflect the views of the publisher, and the publisher hereby disclaims any responsibility for them.

Any people depicted in stock imagery provided by Thinkstock are models, and such images are being used for illustrative purposes only. Certain stock imagery © Thinkstock.

ISBN: 978-1-4917-3637-1 (sc)
ISBN: 978-1-4917-3638-8 (e)

Library of Congress Control Number: 2014909794

Printed in the United States of America.

iUniverse rev. date: 05/28/2014

Dedication

To all the FIFA 2014 Brazil World Cup Soccer Players, who scaled through the stages and made it to the pinnacle of the beautiful game

Acknowledgments

Special thanks and appreciation to Dr. Brian Peacock, my former adult soccer teammate, who generously shared his soccer training notes, comments, philosophy, and training ideas as the foundation for this book. My gratitude also goes to Ms. Shola Alara, who diligently provided proofreading services for the manuscript.

Contents

Dedication v

Acknowledgments vii

Preface xiii

Soccer Matters...xiv

Author's Soccer Background..xv

Chapter 1   Science, Math, and Soccer 1

Chapter 2   Player Positional Placement......................................3

Chapter 3   Spaces, Spots, and Position 5

Field Dimensions..5

Chapter 4   Squashed Squares Formation 7

Squares and Triangles in Offense Choices 8

Defensive Squares..8

Chapter 5   Evolution of Game Plan..10

Player Organization..10

Chapter 6   The Traditional Positions 12

Chapter 7   Modern Positions...14

The 4-3-3 Line-up 15

Chapter 8   New Innovative Line-Ups 16

Chapter 9   Get Moving..18

Chapter 10   The Right Equipment 19

Chapter 11   The Practice Plan 20

Practicing in Pairs 20

Chapter 12   Stopping the Ball 22

Chapter 13   Adjusting to the Big Field 23

Chapter 14   The Fun of Pairing...24

Chapter 15   Using the Squares 25

Opposing squares 26
Chapter 16 Strength, Stamina, and More.................................27
Strength 27
Speed 28
Skill 29
Measuring Skill 29
Chapter 17 The Height of a Kick 32
Chapter 18 The Flare of Dribbling 34
Tips for dribbling 34
A Dozen Hints for Dribbling 35
Chapter 19 Using the Field Scenario 38
Seeing the Field 38
Calling for the Ball...39
Spreading out to Create Space 39
Shooting the Ball..40
Soccer Foot Golf 42
Chapter 20 Situational Set Plays..43
Simple Does It.. 44
Playing It Safe 45
Chapter 21 Goalkeeping 46
Strategy of Play 47
Sharing the Ball..48
Game Simulation 48
Being a Good Sport..48
Chapter 22 The 17 Laws of Soccer...50
Chapter 23 Mathematical Permutations 53
Chapter 24 Player Permutations and Combinations.................56
Permutations 56
Combination 57
Arithmetic Groups and Combinations 58
Fun with Poker Chips and Colored Bibs—Randomization 58
Allocating and Assessing Playing Time......................................59
Using the Sets of Four 60
Counting wins and losses 61
Chapter 25 Using Geometry for Player Lineups 62
Scalene triangle 63
Acute triangle...63
Isosceles triangle...63

Equilateral triangle 64
Obtuse triangle 64
Right triangle 64
Passing and shooting targets 66
The Bigger the Angle the Bigger the Target 67
Assessing Areas 69
Pythagoras' Theorem 71
Vectors and Trajectories 73
Chapter 26 Motion, Force, and Pressure 75
Impact of Forces 76
Pressure 77
Chapter 27 Averages, Differences, and Ratios 79
Probabilities 79
Chapter 28 Body Physiology: Heart, Lung, and Muscles 81
Chapter 29 Moments, Work, and Energy 83
Moment of Inertia 83
Chapter 30 Statics and Dynamics 85
Chapter 31 Math and Science of Time Management 87
Chapter 32 Shapes on the Field 89
Chapter 33 Conclusion: Math Matters for Sports 91

Appendix A: Distance conversion factors 95

Appendix B: Tips and Guides for Ball Control 97

About the author 105

Preface

Soccer is the beautiful game and the most athletic sport that is widely recognized around the world. January 2014 statistics show that over 50 million youth play soccer worldwide. This includes my own three-year-old grandson, who has already learned the art of kicking a soccer ball.

Early training of soccer means a lifetime of love of the sport. The enjoyment of soccer transcends mere involvement as a player, coach, fan, sponsor, dad, mom, or grand-parents. There are subtle lessons of life to be learned from soccer as a team sport. One aspect that is often ignored is the potential to use soccer to teach basic math and science principles, which are essential for later career paths in the technical fields. It is this void that prompted me to write **Youth Soccer Training Slides** as a way to leverage soccer training to spark the interest of kids and adults in the applications of math and science. "Youth Soccer Training Slides: A Math and Science Approach" is a sequel following my first soccer book of 2010 entitled "Physics of Soccer: Using Math and Science to Improve Your Game." That first book was published to coincide with the 2010 FIFA World Cup Tournament Soccer in South Africa. This second book is written to coincide with the 2014 FIFA World Cup Soccer Tournament in Brazil.

Although **Youth Soccer Training Slides** targets youth soccer training, it is quite suitable and recommended for adult soccer training as well. The technical principles are general enough to apply to all levels of soccer training. The presentation slides format of the book makes it amenable for pick-and-choose applications of specific training topics.

The short chapter by chapter approach is intended to encourage youth reading.

Soccer Matters

In his latest 2014 book, the Great Pele of Brazil emphasizes "Why Soccer Matters." In the opinion of this author, soccer, indeed, matters not only because of its socio-economic impacts around the world, but also because of the various other benefits it offers. Soccer matters because it is a thinking game and the ultimate team sport. The theme and premise offered by **Youth Soccer Training Slides** cover various math and science topics to enhance the understanding and facilitate more enjoyment of the game.

Author's Soccer Background

Deji Badiru is an award winning youth and adult soccer coach from 1985 through 1996 in Norman, Oklahoma. He attended Saint Finbarr's College in Lagos, Nigeria in the early 1970s, where he played on the junior school team. He played college soccer at Tennessee Tech University in the mid-1970s and later played adult soccer in Orlando, Florida and Norman, Oklahoma. His older son, Ade, whose soccer photo adorns the front cover, played competitive traveling youth soccer in Oklahoma and has played adult soccer in Michigan for over 15 years. His younger son, TJ, whose soccer photos appear in Chapter 1, played competitive youth traveling soccer in Oklahoma, Tennessee, and Ohio. He also played High School Soccer at Beavercreek High School, where he won several championship awards and accolades.

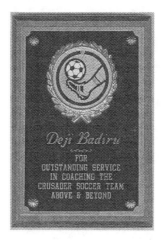

Chapter 1

Science, Math, and Soccer

"An understanding of the basic principles of physics gives a player a better knowledge of the behavior of the soccer ball in relation to game scenarios; thereby creating the ability to play the game more intelligently."

—Deji Badiru, Author of "The Physics of Soccer: Using Math and Science to Improve Your Game," 2010

Soccer is a cerebral sport. The game of soccer has a lot of science and math embedded in it. Science in this context embodies both the natural sciences and the social sciences. The figure below illustrates some of the basic relationships. For example, the rules of soccer represent one aspect of abiding with law and order. Medicine has a lot to do with the physical fitness of a player. Believe it or not, "business" in soccer covers not only the management of the soccer enterprise, but also such things as interpersonal relationships of teammates and intra-team negotiation of passing the ball. The main goal of **Youth Soccer Training Slides** is to sensitize coaches and players to the "thinking" aspect of soccer rather than the "big, brawny, and fast" aspects. More specific details can be obtained from dedicated Math and Science reference books.

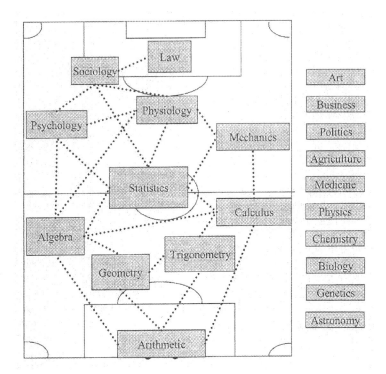

Law
Sociology
Physiology
Psychology
Mechanics
Statistics
Calculus
Algebra
Trigonometry
Geometry
Arithmetic

Art
Business
Politics
Agriculture
Medicine
Physics
Chemistry
Biology
Genetics
Astronomy

Chapter 2

Player Positional Placement

In soccer, player placement is everything. Who goes where is an essential part of covering the entire playing field for both offense and defense. The most successful coaches are those who know how to position their players based on each player's relative skills, speed, interest, availability, enthusiasm, and willingness to adapt. Coaching should be designed to each player's ability and potential. Geometry, the mathematics of size, shape, and relative position of objects, helps in understanding the full utilization of the playing space. In the figure below, the player has to be cognizant of the locations and movements of teammates as well as opponents to take full advantage of the instantaneous scenario of the game at hand.

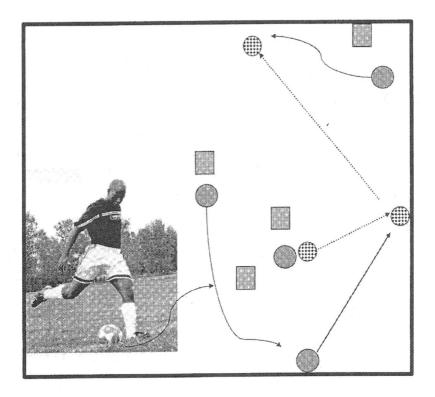

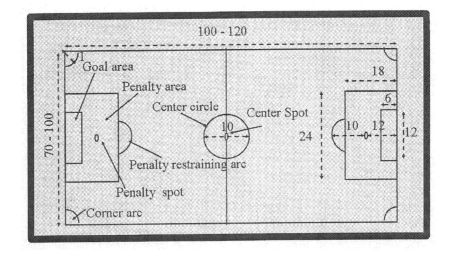

Chapter 3

Spaces, Spots, and Position

Soccer is dynamic. Every player is moving to find a space. The ball is passed into an open space created by player movement.

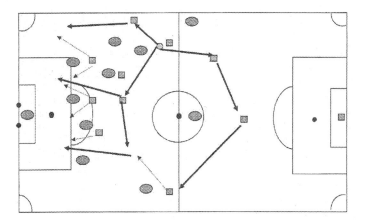

Field Dimensions

The key is to find your space within the soccer field dimensions.

G—Goal—8 yds. by 8 ft.
L—Field Length—100 – 130 yds.

W—Field Width—70 – 100 yds. (Length must be greater than Width)
C—Center Circle—10 yds. radius
PA—Penalty Area—18 yds by 44 yds
GA—Goal Area—6 yds. by 20 yds.
PS—Penalty Spot—12 yds
PRA—Penalty Restraining Arc – 10 yds radius
CA—Corner Arc – 1 yd.

Chapter 4

Squashed Squares Formation

In his coaching and playing days, my former soccer buddy, Brian Peacock, popularized the squashed squares formation for soccer practice. If you ever watch a soccer game – whether it be a hoard of seven-year-olds or national professional teams in the World Cup, you will be able to see how players link together in tactical groups. You will not see perfect squares. Squares sometimes they get a bit squashed and even look more like a "Y", but you should be able to find four players (on each side) in a position to cooperate in the next step of the game.

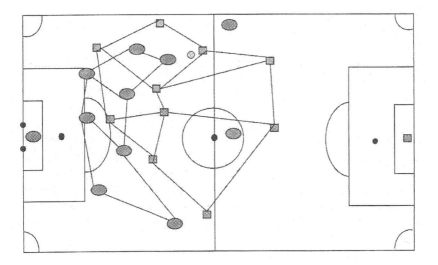

Squares and Triangles in Offense Choices

For many years coaches have talked about triangles, particularly in relation to offense. Triangles give the player with the ball three options – pass the ball to one of his/her teammates or take the ball forward by himself or herself. But what if he or she loses the ball? There should always be a team mate trailing the player with the ball.

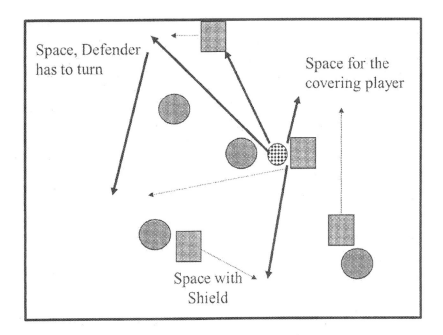

Defensive Squares

Similarly, from the defensive point of view, there should always be someone behind the player who is confronting the player with the ball. In this way we have what systems engineers call redundancy. Other people would call it belt and braces. The other two defensive players do double duty – they cut off passing avenues and position themselves to receive the ball should their teammate obtain possession. So in every play, there should be (at least) four players on each team that have a possibility to contribute to the next step in the game.

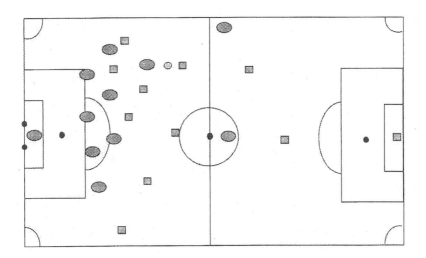

Chapter 5

Evolution of Game Plan

If a game lasts 90 minutes and there are 22 players, then on average each player has the ball for $90/22 = 4.1$ minutes, or less (approximately, 3 minutes), if you subtract the time that the ball is out of play or on its way from one player to the next.

So why are players so tired after a game in which they only play a few minutes? Because the most important player in the game is the one who is going to get the ball next (either on offense or defense). Because you don't always know who that will be, you had better get into a good position to be that person. Although your share of the ball maybe only two or three minutes, your job is to always be involved. The more one player consumes time on the ball (hogs the ball), the less time other players have with the ball.

Player Organization

There are two basic ways of organizing the roles of players on a team – you can have each player assigned to mark a particular opponent or a particular area of the field. However, in practice the game is much more flexible than this and, although players are still assigned to general areas of the field and sometimes to particular opponents, contemporary systems involve the key elements of flexibility and redundancy.

On offense, players look for space and, on defense, players try to fill the space. Soccer is a bit like chess; the players must think two or three moves ahead. They must be ready if a teammate loses the ball, act as decoys to create space and always try to anticipate the next move of a teammate or opponent. The key approach here is systems, flexibility, and redundancy.

Chapter 6

The Traditional Positions

You knew your job by the number on your jersey. You also knew whose job it was to mark you by the number on his shirt. I grew up playing the traditional offensive-minded positions of a soccer game (5-3-2) with five players on offense, two players in mid-field, and three defensive players, as shown in the Figure below.

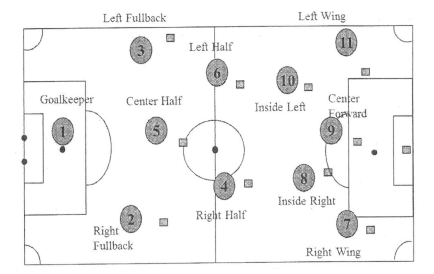

This formation consists of two fullbacks, three midfielders, and five forwards. Coaches of that bygone era lived by the cliché of "the best defense is a good offense." Take the game to the opponent, with five forwards, and you would not have to do much home-base defense.

The backfield consists of the following:

- Left fullback
- Right fullback

The middle consists of the following:

- Left halfback
- Center halfback
- Right halfback

The forward batch in the 2-3-5 formation consists of the following:

- Outside left wing
- Inside left forward
- Center forward
- Inside right forward
- Outside right wing

On defense, keep between your man and the goal. Wing players (wingers), stay wide, but come back for the ball promptly. Center forward, stay up field (but don't get offside). Center half and full back, stay back and mark your man (or woman). Inside forwards and wing halves must run, run, and run . . . and keep running. Sprinting is a particularly desirable ability of offensive soccer players.

Chapter 7

Modern Positions

The modern line-up of soccer players use what is called 4-2-4 and its variants. The numbers don't mean anything anymore. The sweeper plays behind a defensive wall of four. The wingers and center forward stay up. Full backs overlap on offense, mid-fielders take on the player with the ball, and wingers come back for the ball. Fullbacks overlap. Sweeper plays behind (or in front) of the back row of 3 defenders. Dual strikers play the ball back to their teammate. Midfielders intercept and distribute the ball.

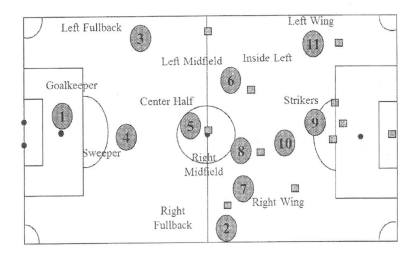

The 4-3-3 Line-up

The 4-3-3 line-up of soccer players follows an increasingly defensive mentality. In this case, more defensive players are assigned to the back of the field. The notion is that if we can prevent the opponent from scoring, we will have a better chance of winning. All we need is just one goal at the opposing end of the field.

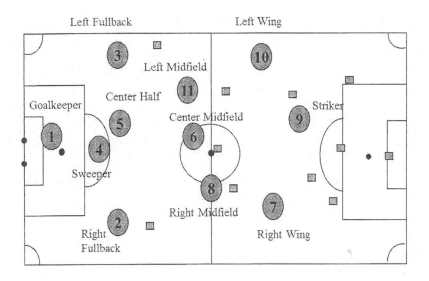

Chapter 8

New Innovative Line-Ups

Danny Blanchflower (10 February 1926 – 9 December 1993) was a famous Irish footballer. Once he was asked by a journalist why he thought that his team had just won an important soccer match. He thought for a while and then responded, expressing pride in his team's offensive power:

"Perhaps it was because we scored more goals than the other side."

His modern counterpart would have said emphatically, expressing pride in his team defensive prowess:

"Because the other side scored less than we did."

Player line-ups have changed again in the attempt to gain an advantage over the opponent by scoring more goals. In one innovative line-up, two rows of defenders – the front row takes the player with the ball, the second row act as sweepers. On-offense players rotate and keep possession until they spot or create a mismatch. The layout below illustrates the line-up, which some people refer to as the Berlin Wall.

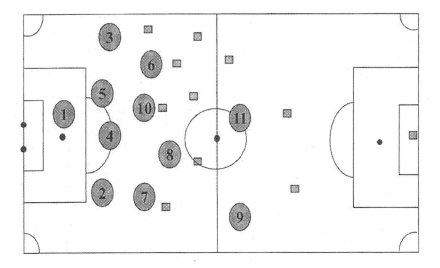

Chapter 9

Get Moving

Players should not stand in line at practice. In practice, as in a game, all players should be moving into a position to be the next participant in a developing situation. That is how you learn the essential "feel" for the game. The best players in the world are always on their toes during a game. Being constantly mobile means they are always ready to spring into game action instantaneously.

When I was a little boy we only had one ball (often a tennis ball or some round rubber ball) and various numbers of players from one to twenty-two. We rarely "practiced"– we just picked teams and played. If you were on your own, you used the wall to play against or a target to shoot at. When there were more players, it was often useful to assign general areas of responsibility around the field, but woe betide anyone who said he played on offense or defense. The difference between offence and defense has nothing to do with the particular players – it all depends which side has the ball. If your side has the ball everybody is on offense and should be expecting the ball to come their way. Similarly, if the other side has the ball then everybody is on defense – that is moving into a position to prevent opponents from doing their job – trying to be in a position to be the next participant in the game. The bottom line is, don't stand around. Get moving and fix your eyes on the ball and your teammates.

Chapter 10

The Right Equipment

The ideal equipment for a practice session is one ball and one cone for each player or two and four sets of four different colored practice jerseys or bibs. There are many ways of making use of four sets of four different colored bibs. You can have greens, blues, yellows, and reds playing together; you can have two reds play two greens or three yellows and a blue, and so on. The coach with an imagination can mix up the players in many different ways for different exercises and mini games.

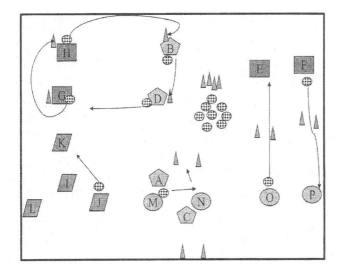

Chapter 11

The Practice Plan

Almost every kind of practice session can involve groups of two, four, eight or sixteen players. Sixteen players are enough for any team; any more reduces playing time to unreasonable levels. Back in the old days, substitutes were unheard of – you played all the game and if someone got hurt you played with ten.

Practicing in Pairs

The first exercise should involve pairs of players just kicking the ball to each other, with their right and left feet at varying distances apart – from about 5 to 20 meters (1 meter = 3.2808 feet) and then back to 5 meters. Just keep the ball moving until each player has kicked the ball at least fifty times. You don't really have to teach children of any age how to kick a ball; if they do it often enough they will learn. It may be useful to put a cone in between each pair so that the players can aim at it, around it, or over it. You don't have to pick up the cone every time it gets knocked over, it won't run away and will still be a good target.

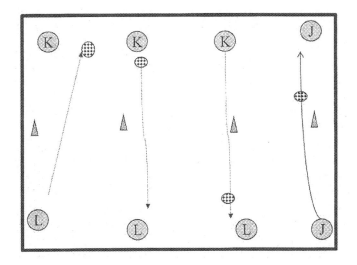

The next variation on this pairs game is to have the players move around their cone in circles of different sizes and in different directions. This way, passers will learn to pass the ball in front of a moving teammate, which is most important when the game gets going for real. A variation is to have the pairs move up and down the field passing the ball to each other. This way they will learn for themselves that the game is much easier if they use both feet.

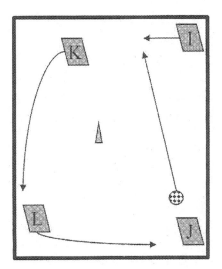

Chapter 12

Stopping the Ball

Now with all this kicking going on, we didn't mention stopping the ball. Well it just happened without us thinking about it. It does not matter how you stop the ball, provided you don't use your hands. If you do it often enough you will learn to do it well. You will also learn to link stopping the ball with kicking it.

Just playing a game in pairs passing, throwing or punting the ball to each other at distances varying from 5 to 30 yards and more will give players plenty of practice at stopping the ball, especially if you make a competition in which the first pair to 50 kicks wins. This way you will get hard low balls straight at the player, balls that the player has to run for, bouncing balls and high balls. They will use their feet, knees and chest. But most of all they will learn to link stopping the ball with pushing it forward for the next action.

Chapter 13

Adjusting to the Big Field

A fun pairs game is to start facing each other about 20 meters apart and kicking the ball alternately with the object of getting the ball over the opponent's goal line. This teaches the players how to kick the ball hard and long, and makes them run. More about the big "S" – Stamina later. Oh, by the way you can allow the players to punt or throw the ball instead of kicking it.

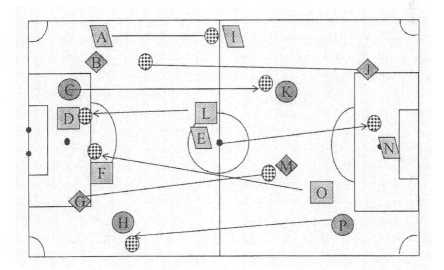

Chapter 14

The Fun of Pairing

Still in pairs, the players can learn about dribbling and tackling. If there is only one cone between two players they can alternate defending and attacking the cone. Two cones, placed 10 or 20 yards apart can become two goals. The first to reach10 wins.

There's even more to this pairs stuff. When the coach blows the whistle, players change partners and carry on with their kicking, passing, stopping, running, dribbling, tackling and shooting games. Before you know where you are, the practice session will be over, every player will be tired, they will have kicked the ball a few hundred times, they will be a little better at the game, they will have had a lot of fun, they have only had to think about one other player and nobody had to stand in line.

Here's a fun game. Line the players up facing each other in pairs about 20 yards apart, one ball between each pair, a cone next to each player. The game is to knock down your opponent's cone. Every few minutes, stop the game, move each player one position to the left (or right) and then continue. The end player will have to cross to the other side. Don't worry about knocked down cones they will not run away. Keep the play moving. Try the game with the cones further apart. This will make players run.

Chapter 15

Using the Squares

For this activity you need 4 players, one ball, and 2 or 4 cones. It might be useful to select 2 players with one color bib and the other 2 with another, but it doesn't really matter. You start by making a small square – about 5 yards across and have the players keep the ball moving in any direction around and across the square, first time kicking or stopping with one foot and kicking with the other. You can alternate which foot does what, but the key is to keep the ball moving. Put the cones in the middle and have the players kick around or over them. Enlarge the size of the square, but keep the ball moving. Have the players pass the ball and then move to another corner of the square. Keep the ball moving. Enlarge the square again. Keep the ball moving. You get the idea. Ten minutes of this and each player will have stopped and kicked the ball a whole bunch of times and would have worked his or her heart just like it should be working in a game.

Now take turns putting one of the four in the middle to act as a passive defender. The other three keep the ball away from the player in the middle and keep the ball moving. The player in the middle doesn't tackle or even try to intercept, he just gives the others something to think about. Later the player in the middle becomes more aggressive and tries to intercept. But don't forget to keep the ball moving and use both feet. By the way change the player in the middle from time to time.

Make two goals about 20 yards apart – a single cone will do. Play 2 on 2. After a few minutes rotate the pairs so that they play against other opponents. Keep the ball moving. Run off the ball into a clear position for your partner to pass to you. Try dribbling around your opponent every now and again.

Stop the play; tell every player to race around the goal post at the end of the field and then back to their playing position. There's nothing like sprinting and racing to get the blood moving to create some fun.

Opposing squares

Play four on four mini games. Think about getting into position to receive the ball and don't forget the trailing player – behind the man with the ball and the man who is confronting the man with the ball. Every few minutes blow the whistle and ask each player to say what he or she is doing and where he/she is going next. This is called "heads up football". It makes the players think about the squares and about how the game is happening. If you do this too often the players will complain that you are interrupting their fun. A great lesson for coaches – allow the players to play and keep out of the way most of the time. Remember that with 8 players in a mini game each player only gets the ball about 1/8-th of the time but should be running all of the time. This 4-on-4 level is probably the optimal level of competition. Don't forget to swap the teams around so that the mini teams play against different opponents and with different teammates. But keep reminding them of the importance of moving off the ball and covering the player with the ball. Once the players have mastered this kind of competition they are ready to go.

Chapter 16

Strength, Stamina, and More

Strength and stamina go hand in hand – the exercises like running, jumping, skipping, stopping and starting make your legs strong. You need strong legs to kick the ball far. Probably the best way to develop the strength to kick the ball far is by kicking the ball a long way a lot of times. It is great fun to have kicking competitions in pairs or fours – kick the ball alternately and try to move your opponent back to his own goal line. Alternate between the left foot and the right foot. By way of a change, punt or throw the ball – one hand or two hands. Don't always run forward. Try backward and skipping sideways. Walk on all fours – either facing up or down. Play "crab football." Jump as high as you can – at least ten or more times.

There are other ways of developing strength, but they all require dedicated practice. Squats, sit-ups and push-ups are all familiar and have a place in any strength training routine. If you can reach the cross bar or there is a jungle gym close by add in pull-ups. Be careful that the goal doesn't fall over.

Strength

Physical strength is the science of overcoming the resistance of a force. Strength measurement is the mathematics of assessing the magnitude of the resistance that is overcome. Strength training involves resisted muscular activity and what better resistance is there other than your playing buddy, provided you are about the same size. Do arm wrestling. Have pushing and pulling competitions. Lift and carry your partner. Do squats with your partner on your back. Have push up and sit up competitions. Try squat thrusts and burpees – bend your knees, touch the floor and then jump up as high as you can – at least ten times. Then progress to: bend your knees, hands on the floor, jump your legs backward then forward and then jump up and repeat, repeat, repeat.

Just look at how strong the pros are. They can kick or throw the ball more than half the length of the field. Strength rules, but it all comes from practice again and again.

Speed

The difference between top players and those less gifted or practiced is the speed with which they do things. They get to the ball quicker, they control the ball quicker, they kick the ball faster and they seem to be able to think faster. One practical example of the advantage of speed is that the first player to the ball usually wins the tackle. Another is that the first player into an open space provides a good target for a passer. Finally, the fastest runner will move around and away from an opponent and into open space more quickly. Speed is important but sometimes the cliché "more haste, less speed applies." You should always have your brain in gear before you set your feet in motion! But this takes practice.

There are two basic measures of human performance – accuracy and speed. Accuracy means that you achieve your objective and speed means that you do it quickly. Sometimes there are speed – accuracy tradeoffs. Most children of all ages like to run races, because it is usually clear who the winner is and, because most people eventually come across someone faster than themselves, losing isn't a big deal – it just makes you try harder next time, or chose the right opponents.

In practice, coaches should make use of races to improve speed. The races may be of any distance – from 5 yards to the length of the pitch. They can involve turns around the cones or shuttle runs. They can be forwards, sideways or backwards. They can use two feet or hands and feet. They can involve jumps, swerves, falling down and getting up. They can even involve the ball. You can kick the ball, with one or alternating feet. You can kick it a long way ahead or keep close control. For a change you can carry the ball or throw it up in the air and catch it. Races can involve two or more players. Shuttle runs, ball control runs, and reciprocal passing races at various distances apart. Races rule. They are fun. And races develop speed in all aspects of the game. Even the coach can join in. Most practices should include races of one kind or another. They are intrinsically motivating.

Skill

This is what it is all about. All players have skills, but some have more than others. Some have different skills. Soccer skill is about connecting your brain to your feet, via a whole bunch of neural connections. There is a simple truism about skill – the more you practice the more skillful you will become at the thing you are practicing. In fact, it is possible to continue to improve speed and accuracy over millions of practice cycles. But there is a complication. It is possible to learn bad habits and repeat mistakes. It is also possible to focus on just a few skills to the exclusion of others. Good players have a wide variety of skills and can play in any position. There is one famous exception that proves this rule. One of the greatest players of all time – Stanley Mathews (English player, 1 Feb 1915 – 23 Feb 2000)—couldn't (or didn't) kick the ball with his left foot, rarely headed the ball and hardly ever scored a goal. But he was a brilliant right-winger, who regularly tied the left full back in knots and, to use a term that postdates his era, was responsible for many "assists."

Measuring Skill

How can you measure skill? There are two ways – accuracy and speed. Accuracy means that you do what you planned to do – like scoring a goal, making a successful pass, getting the ball under control or tackling an opponent. Speed is measured by the time it takes to do these things. The complicating thing about skill is that the transaction usually has to be completed in the context of opponents, ground, and weather conditions. It's one thing to be able to juggle the ball with your feet, head and knees a hundred times; it is an altogether different challenge to receive a high ball with your back to the goal and a defender close behind you, chest it down, turn and shoot past the advancing goalkeeper. There are two theories about the acquisition of skill. The first is that you learn the elements individually, then put them together and finally do them under game conditions. The alternative theory is that you practice game situations and the skills are acquired incidentally. The author believes that the latter approach is more fun and therefore likely to be more successful in the long run.

There really are only four kinds of skill in soccer – ball control, tackling, kicking, and strategic use of these elements. Ball control skills involve the process of receiving the ball from any direction and at any height and at any speed, dribbling it and preparing to pass or shoot the ball. Tackling is all about timing. There are a few guidelines that are worth mentioning up front. Watch the ball not your opponent's feet or eyes. Either get in quickly before your opponent has control of the ball or hang back a little and wait for your opponent to give it to you. Surprisingly the latter strategy is often the most successful. The kicking skill is basic and can only be acquired through practice, practice, practice. You can kick the ball with any part of your foot – inside, top, outside, toe or heel – they all have their place. Kicking skills are best learned through mini games of shooting and passing, not by listening to the coach tell you how to kick.

The square is a good way of practicing ball control skills. The four players should just pass the ball about as the square gets bigger and smaller and changes shape, rotates and progresses around the field. The key rule to this practice of ball control and kicking skills is to tell the players that the ball must not stop. You can play first time passing or two or three touch. As the control skills develop, players will control the ball and move it into a position for the next pass all in one movement. A fun game is to have one of the four players act as a passive defender in the middle while the others move about and keep the ball in motion. It's surprising how often a passive defender will get the ball on an interception. A progression of this game is to allow the defender to become more aggressive, but then you will often find that it is easier for the three to keep the ball away.

Chapter 17

The Height of a Kick

Now to kicking. As mentioned earlier, the ball may be kicked with any part of the foot, but players will usually get more distance and accuracy if they use the "instep" – the top inner side of the foot. Generally, the non-kicking foot is placed next to the ball, and the head and shoulders are over the ball. But kicking a football is like hitting a golf ball – there are many variations on the theme. If you want the ball to go hard and low you put your body over the ball. If you want to lift it in the air you should approach the ball at an angle of up to 45 degrees. You place your planted foot a little further away, you lean back a little, and you undercut the ball. You can make the ball swerve by hitting it with the outside or inside of the foot. Players should practice all of these variations as they pass the ball around the square. Perhaps the best kicking practice is a one-on-one or two-on-two, in which the teams kick the ball alternately with the aim of getting the ball to the other goal line. One thing to remember is that if the ball is passed along the ground, it makes the receiver's ball control task much easier than if the ball is bouncing.

Assume that you are going to kick the ball straight up in the air. For the time being, assume that there is no air resistance. Your partner has a stop watch which he starts when you kick the ball and stops when the ball hits the ground. The ball height calculation is done as follows:

h = the height
t = the time the ball takes to reach its highest location

u = the initial velocity of the ball just after it has left your foot

Let u = 30 ft/sec

When the ball reaches its highest point, velocity, v = 0

g = the acceleration / deceleration due to gravity

g = 32.2 ft/sec^2 or 9.81 m/s^2

Note that gravity is "negative" as the ball goes up and "positive" as it comes down.

Equations of motion

1. $h = ut + 1/2\ gt^2$
2. $v^2 = u^2 + 2gh$
3. $v = u + gt$
4. Using equation 3 $0 = 30 - 32.2\ t$; $t = 30/32.2$ seconds
5. Using equation 2 $0 = 900 - 2 * 32.2 * h$; h = 13.98 feet
6. Using equation 1 $h = 0 + ½\ 32.2\ t^2$; h = 13.98 feet

The ball will take the same amount of time to come down as it did to go up and when it hits the ground it will be traveling at the same speed as it started.

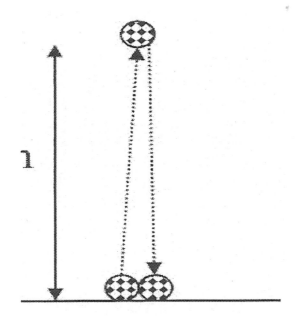

Chapter 18

The Flare of Dribbling

Dribbling is, no doubt, the most fascinating skill in soccer. The player kicks and maneuvers the ball deftly down the field as he tries to get by the opposing players. This is one of the areas where the physics of motion (of the player and ball) is most evident.

Tips for dribbling

- Keep your eyes on the ball,
- Survey where you want the ball to go next,

- Change your direction in an instant,
- Use body fakes,
- Make use of the tightest open space,
- Don't dribble for too long, pass the ball promptly to someone else,
- Don't attempt to dribble everyone; you will eventually lose the ball,
- Dribble the ball over the shortest possible time,
- Dribbling should not be done for sake of just dribbling,
- Use dribbling to advance the ball toward scoring a goal,
- Keep successive dribbling "victims" to not more than two.

A Dozen Hints for Dribbling

The physics of a body in motion sets the stage for executing dribbling moves. Several basic principles of physics apply directly in dribbling. These include momentum, force, energy transfer, body dynamics, mass, kinetic energy, potential energy, center of gravity shifts, and so on. The hints below all have physics of motion as the underlying foundation. The idea here is not to scare readers with too much physics talk. It suffices to know that physics makes most of the hints below possible. For better dribbling, do the following.

1. Shift your body (and center of gravity) to one side. By bending the body on one side the defender thinks that you are going in that direction, but you have to push the ball in the other direction and adjust your posture to retain the ball.

2. Practice with a smaller ball. One good way to get good at dribbling is to use a small ball, the smaller the better. With a small ball, you will get used to the constant adjustments needed to control the small ball. When you play with a full-sized ball later on, you will find it much easier.

3. Use all the surfaces of your foot. Most often you will be using the front part of your instep, especially when you are dribbling at a fast speed. To become a good dribbler, you must learn to

use the outside and inside of both feet. This way you can cut the ball away from a defender.

4. Touch the ball with each step you take with the ball. In very quick succession, touch the ball a little bit ahead of you when you dribble. This will create both good control and increase your dribbling speed with the ball. With this kind of control you can elude defenders when they try to reach in and steal the ball, you can just cut the ball away since it is always so close to you. It is almost as if you are trying to get as many touches in as you dribble forward with the ball.

5. Change the pace and direction often. This is the key to going past a defender while dribbling. You don't necessarily need to be extremely fast to beat someone on the dribble; rather, you need to lull the defender to commit in one direction or the other for a second and then break past the defender with a burst of speed before he or she realizes what just happened.

6. Keep your head up and eyes from the ground. Maintain your awareness of the surroundings as you retain your focus on the ball while dribbling. Look up slightly so you know if someone is making a run, another defender is approaching, or there is space to attack.

7. Practice often to improve your weak foot. The best advice is just to use it. If you continue to kick the ball against a wall with your weaker foot, slowly but steadily you will improve the foot's proficiency and power.

8. Bloat your posture to use your body to protect the ball. Shield the ball with your body when a defender gets close. Try to keep the ball on the foot that is farthest from the defender and your body protects the ball.

9. Be unpredictable on your feet while surprising the opponent. Dribble in one direction, fake a shot in the other direction while dribbling, and suddenly shift to the other direction.

10. Practice dribbling with a buddy. Practice again and again.

11. Tap rather than kick the ball when dribbling. In some cases, you can drag or push the ball along the ground in one direction or the other without losing contact with the ball.

12. Learn the physics of body movement and use it to your advantage.

Chapter 19

Using the Field Scenario

Situational awareness (SA) is a key aspect of fully leveraging whatever the field of play has to offer. Always scan the field and adjust your actions accordingly.

Seeing the Field

Great players have "eyes in the back of their heads." In technical terms, they have good situational awareness. Players should practice looking around and listening to their teammates calling for the ball. One way of encouraging situational awareness skills is for the coach to blow the whistle to stop play during practice games. Each player then has to say what he is going to do next and what the other players (teammates or opponents) are going to do next. Players should be encouraged to play 'with their heads up." The next part of seeing is anticipating – predicting where your teammates and opponents are going to move in the next few seconds. The skill of anticipating and predicting the action of other players is not only good for playing soccer, it is also useful for non-sports applications, such as defensive driving. If you can anticipate and predict the actions of other drivers, you can proactively plan your own actions to avoid a collision.

Calling for the Ball

Shouting on the field is a good way to get the attention of teammates. In addition to using shouting to call for the ball, it can also be used to alert teammates to an opponent approaching from a blind spot. A natural partner to seeing is shouting or using other signals to attract the attention of a teammate. A potential receiver should shout the name of the ball player as he moves into position. Alternatively, a third player should shout the name of an open receiver. Pointing, raising your hand, and making eye contact with a teammate are good ways of helping. There is a fine line between legal tactical shouting and "verbal obstruction." You should always shout a name and not things like "my ball" or "square ball." You should not shout if you are not in an open position. Shouting that is aimed at deceiving the opposition may be penalized.

Spreading out to Create Space

The effective use of space is the most important tactical part of the game. Space is where you or a teammate is and your opponent is not. When you get more advanced in your analysis, space is where you, your teammate or the ball is going to be in the next few seconds. In the early days of traditional formation (i.e., two full backs three half backs and five forwards), the players had fairly rigid territories. But as the game has progressed the job of a player is not to cover his designated opponent or area of the field. Rather, it is to move strategically with the play. Strive to move into an open space and always remember the need to cover the player who has the ball.

Whatever the basic lineup is adopted, players will find themselves participating in various squares that cover the field. A typical situational square will include the player with the ball, two teammates within a fairly close passing distance and a fourth player behind him. A change in the direction of the play will find players participating in a different square. The defensive counterpart of the offensive square is that there should always be a player between an offensive player and the goal.

Three-on-one or two-on-two games are very good ways of making players find space. Again it is often good to play with passive defense – the team without the ball doesn't tackle – they just look for interceptions. The passer should pass the ball in front of a moving teammate. Good players like an opponent to commit to a tackle – it gives them a better opportunity to dribble around the opponent or pass the ball. Here is one thing on slide tackling, which is a very important part of the game at the right moment. You must get the ball and not the player. You must also remember that you will end up on the ground and, therefore, and may be out of the game if your tackle is not successful.

As players become more experienced, space can be created by decoys and strategic shielding, which is placing your body between your opponent and the ball. But pushing off will get you called for an obstruction.

Shooting the Ball

Shooting at the goal is the occasional end result of a long build up around the field and, because it is so occasional, it is important not to squander the opportunity. The trick is to increase the probability of a successful outcome, which is to score a goal. The first rule of shooting is to get close enough to the goal. The closer you are, the better your chance of scoring. It is rare for children to score from outside the penalty area because they can't kick the ball hard enough or far enough. Even the professionals only have a 50-50 chance of scoring from outside the box if the goalkeeper is in a good position to see the ball coming. There are two reasons for not shooting from too far away – space and time. The space thing is that the target – the goal is relatively smaller the further you are away – so that a good shot from close up will go just inside the post and the one with the same angular direction from further away will miss the goal. The second problem is time – the more time you give the goalkeeper to see the ball coming and move into its path, the more likely it is that he or she will save it. Therefore, the first rule of shooting is "get within range!"

The second rule is to choose as big a target as possible so as to reduce the chance of missing the goal and the chance of the goalkeeper stopping the ball. The target is the space around the goalkeeper – above and to the side – but within the goal posts. Note that it is generally harder for a goal keeper to reach a low ball than a high one – it takes him a longer time to dive and move his hands to the bottom two feet of the goal than to the upper six feet – assuming that the goalkeeper is six feet tall. But if small children play in full-size goals, then it makes sense to kick the ball over the goalkeeper's head. If the goalkeeper advances to "narrow the angle" then you should shoot towards the side with the biggest gap – often the far post. When you become very good at the game you may be able to lob the ball over the head of the advancing goalkeeper. However, this takes a lot of practice. You have to learn to control the trajectory by hitting the ball just hard enough. Otherwise, the ball will go over the crossbar.

As the player becomes more skillful at kicking, he will become more adept at "bending" the ball around the advancing goalkeeper. If you want to swerve the ball to the right hit it with the outside of your right foot or the inside of the left foot and vice versa. One more thing; if you want the ball to dip then you hit the ball with the inside of the foot with a glancing upward blow – so as to impart a top spin on the ball.

The ball is rarely stationary when the player is about to shoot, except for a penalty kick or a free kick. The shooter has more time to prepare for his shot if the ball is rolling toward him than if it is delivered from the side or behind. Thus, the golden rule for the assisting a player is to play the ball back to the shooter or if there is sufficient space between the shooter and the goalkeeper, to place the ball in front of the shooter so that he can run on to it. This kind of a pass has a low probability of success because the advancing goalkeeper will have more chance to come out of his goal and narrow the angle. It is difficult for a player to receive a ball from behind but it is even more difficult to receive a bouncing ball because the shooter will have to time his movement to the ball more precisely and may have to control the ball first and then shoot.

Shooting, like any skill, can only be improved by practice, practice and more practice. There is no value for a dozen or so players standing in line waiting for their turn to shoot. Perhaps the best form of shooting practice is in groups of four players. Place two cones to make a goal post, have one player act as goalkeeper, two in front and one behind and practice passing and shooting none stop. Rotate the players frequently. With this practice layout, it is possible to demonstrate the effectiveness of different forms of assist – coming back towards the shooter, coming from behind and bouncing. Another level of practice is to have one of the pair in front of the goal provide passive defense so that the shooter has to move sideways to get a clear shot at the goal. If he scores and then the goalkeeper can turn and provide passive defense for the new shooter that was standing on the other side of the goal.

Soccer Foot Golf

Another fun way to practice shooting a soccer ball effectively is to use a foot golf layout. This is where a 21-inch hole (or depression) is dug into the ground for the purpose of players kicking a ball into it from various distances and alternate angles. It is fun and effective. Practice competition can be built around this layout.

Chapter 20

Situational Set Plays

Situations that develop during a soccer game offer opportunities for set plays. There are quite a few stoppages in soccer – when the ball goes out of bounds, when a foul has been committed or when the game starts or restarts after a goal. Quite a few strategies have been tried after a kick off. One interesting one is to kick the ball as far forward as possible – of course this gives the ball to the opposition, but at least the play will be continued toward the other team's goal. The more common and conservative tactic is to retain possession by passing the ball to a teammate standing close by, who in turn passes the ball back to a half back; then the midfield possession game can start. There are other more risky and innovative starts – pass the ball directly to a winger, dribble the ball up field or a pass back followed by a kick up field to attackers that have had time to run into a position where they have at least a fifty-fifty chance of receiving the ball. Note that the ball must travel forward from the kick off. This rule is an anachronism and really serves no useful purpose.

Before the change in rules regarding goal (dead ball) kicks, it was common for the goalkeeper to pass the ball sideways to a fullback, who then returns it to the goalkeeper. The goalkeeper would then advance to the edge of the penalty box, bouncing the ball every four steps, before kicking it up field. Nowadays, this tactic is not allowed and is not really an issue, except for young children as the balls used nowadays have a much greater coefficient of restitution and can be kicked much further than the old soggy leather balls. Also nowadays, goal keepers can usually reach at least the half way line with a goal kick and often well into the opponents half with a punt. A few other things have changed – mostly for the better. Those heavy soggy balls would not bounce well on a soft muddy goalmouth – this gave rise to all sorts of odd situations and encouraged attackers to confront the goalkeeper. Indeed, charges on the goalkeeper used to be allowed and even encouraged. Clever attackers would stand in front and slightly to one side of the goalkeeper so that he couldn't punt the ball with his preferred foot – usually the right one. A big no-no was raising your foot in front of the goalkeeper.

Simple Does It

KISS – Keep it simple sweetheart! Is good advice. A high probability pass into good space is better than a 50-50 ball to a teammate, who is closely marked or a long hopeful kick up field. But, when the ball is in your own penalty area, don't play around with it, get it out of there. In the old days, a pass back to the goalkeeper was an important and perfectly legitimate way of playing safe. But some teams abused this strategy in order to waste time. So, the law was changed to disallow the goalkeeper from using his hands to pick up a direct pass (with the foot) from a team mate. This doesn't mean that you shouldn't pass back, only that you run a greater risk of losing the ball if you do. But remember always pass back wide of the goal, in case the goalkeeper misses the ball.

Wherever possible pass the ball to a team mate along the ground, because a bouncing ball is harder to bring under control. Shoot from in front of the goal and not from a narrow angle. If you are out towards the wing and approaching the goal – pass the ball back toward a teammate running into the penalty area – he will have a better chance of scoring than you.

Passing the ball is usually better than trying to dribble it around an opponent, unless that opponent is not covered, in which case you have more space to play with. Don't try to develop complex sequences – remember that fours are about as much as we can handle mentally.

Playing It Safe

Playing safe, particularly on defense, is of great importance. Clear the ball out of your own penalty area. Don't pass across your own goal in your half of the field – this will often lead to an interception and no defensive cover. Pass to a close teammate who is not marked. Play the game in your opponent's half of the field.

Always have someone covering the player with the ball – usually about 5 to 10 yards so that if he is tackled there is a good chance that the covering player will be able to regain possession quickly. Forwards are responsible for defense – they must come back and cover behind the player who is challenging for the ball. There is usually no hurry to get up field, unless you have drawn the opponent's defense out of position.

Unless you are a genius, try to get the ball under control before you do something else. Pass to a close-by teammate who is not marked. Pass into clear space but don't provide 50-50 passes and get your teammate creamed.

Chapter 21

Goalkeeping

Goalkeepers save the ball. Goalkeeping is a special skill. It relies on anticipation and agility. The key is to narrow the angle. The key to effective goalkeeping is to provide the smallest possible target to the opposing players by advancing off your goal line. But be careful not to come out too quickly or too far, as this will provide your opponent with the chance to lob the ball over your head. Always cover your near post when the attack is coming from a wing. Keep your legs together or go down on one knee to provide a solid wall. When going out to meet an opponent that is in the clear, dive sideways to block as much of the goal as possible.

Catch the ball rather than punch it. From corner kicks start on the far post and move out and forward toward the ball – you don't want to let it go over your head. Remember that if the ball is in the goal area you should consider it yours.

A good goalkeeper (goalie) can serve as the "quarterback" of a soccer game because he or she has a full view of the field from a vantage point and can direct the play. Since the play often starts with the goalkeeper, he or she can direct the starting distribution of the ball. Distribute the ball to a player that is in the clear. It is often better to throw the ball to an unmarked player out towards the wing rather than kicking the ball up filed. Also, look for a winger who is coming back for the ball close to the half way line – he will often be unmarked. Another ploy is for a mid-fielder to run into space towards the touch line, thus providing a large unmarked target area. .

As the last resort or when you have the wind behind you, kick the ball down field as far as you can. Such a kick is especially effective on hard grounds when the ball bounces high.

Strategy of Play

There are three levels of control of a game. Ball control is executing the basic skills like kicking, dribbling, and tackling. Tactical play is like creating space and passing in to space and using the wind, sun and ground conditions to your advantage. Finally, there is the strategic play, which is carrying out pre-planned attacking moves and defensive cover. Play on your own team's strengths and the opposing team's weaknesses.

Play long balls into the wind and square balls when the wind is behind you in your opponents half – this will prevent you from giving the advancing goalkeeper an easy job. Curl the ball into the goal with the wind from the wing and use the wind to make the ball move away from the goalkeeper. Present the goalkeeper with high bouncing balls on hard grounds. Play long balls over the head of the opposing fullback into space for your winger to run to. Pull the ball back for a teammate who is following up. Never give the goalkeeper an easy ball to intercept or catch.

Overlap by rotating the cover player out towards the wing while making sure that someone else fills in behind the player with the ball. . Forwards run out toward the wing to spread the defense, thus creating large holes. Get into a position for a pass. Come back and wide for a throw from your goalkeeper. Send a player up field as a decoy while another comes across for the ball.

Sharing the Ball

The biggest misdeed in soccer is to hold on to the ball when a teammate is in a better position to shoot or progress up the field. Soccer is a game of sharing. There are super stars, but the best players are those who are team players. Running off the ball, covering a player who has moved up field, providing a good target for a pass, not shouting when you are in a marked position are all good ways that the player without the ball can share – and help the player with the ball to share. There are other ways of sharing – warning a teammate of an opponent behind him, always getting back to help the defense when you have lost the ball, congratulating a teammate who makes a good play – shoot, tackle, run into space or pass. And most of all, be quick to forgive and forget mistakes made by a teammate. After all, nobody intends to make a mistake and your turn may be next.

Game Simulation

It is easy to simulate the game with poker chips on a table. Work on set plays and defensive and offensive strategies. Always look for the squares, with one player trailing the player with the ball. Show how decoys and overlaps create space.

Being a Good Sport

Soccer is a great game and a good sport. And the players, coaches, officials, and spectators should be "good sports." If you play long enough, you will win a few games and loose a few, especially if you progress or gravitate to your own skill level. Of course, the purpose is always to win, but if you won every time you would soon lose interest in the game because there would be no challenge and, therefore, no sport. If you foul an opponent deliberately, stop the ball with your hands, or protest a referee's decision, you are missing the whole point of the game. Coaches, referees, and teammates should be particularly vigilant regarding the following bad behaviors—jersey pulling, errant elbows, deliberate tripping, pushes in the back, tackling through the ball, charging or kicking the goalkeeper, shouting to distract an opponent or, in other ways, acting offensively. Do not retaliate, this will usually get you in a bigger trouble than the initial offense; do not argue with officials, referees, coaches, opponents or spectators – they all usually do their best to play the game. Remember that referees may often play the advantage rule and, thus, ignore even a deliberate foul. Do not criticize your teammates' mistakes. Coaches, don't tell the player that he messed up – he didn't intend to and probably feels bad enough already without your help. Soccer is a game of skill and serendipity. Sometimes the play goes as intended, but more often it doesn't.

Chapter 22

The 17 Laws of Soccer

There are 17 Conventional Laws governing the game of soccer:

1. The field of play
2. The ball
3. The number of players
4. Player's equipment
5. Referees
6. Linesmen
7. Duration of the game
8. The start of play
9. Ball in and out of play
10. Method of scoring
11. Fouls and misconduct
12. Free kick (direct and indirect)
13. Penalty kick
14. Throw in
15. Goal kick
16. Corner kick
17. Hand ball

Most of these laws don't really matter and don't often make sense to players. But if you want to avoid field arguments, you should read the laws and the interpretations. Why?

Laws are general guidelines that are intended to provide some order in the game and provide safety for the players. The "decisions" or rules are much more rigid interpretations that are needed to resolve disagreements regarding the laws. But millions of children all over the world play very happily by interpreting the laws (which they have never read) with common sense.

The "field" is any fairly flat surface with one or two goals. The size of the field and goals depend on how many players there are, how big the players are and how big the ball is. A regular tennis ball on a patch of concrete provides a venue for endless soccer fun. Even law #12 "Fouls and Misconduct" is really common sense. Don't use your hands and be sure to kick the ball not your opponent.

Even in the top level of soccer the job of the officials is to keep the game moving and only interfere when a player may gain an unfair advantage by contravening one of the laws. But people play the game and people are competitive and like structure, especially when it is important which team wins. So we are stuck with all these interpretations.

The "field" is any fairly flat surface with one or two goals. The size of the field and goals depend on how many players there are, how big the players are and how big the ball is. A regular tennis ball on a patch of concrete provides a venue for endless soccer fun. Even law #12 "Fouls and Misconduct" is really common sense. Don't use your hands and kick the ball not your opponent.

Even in the top level of soccer, the job of the officials is to keep the game moving and only interfere when a player may gain an unfair advantage by contravening one of the laws. But people play the game and people are competitive and like structure, especially when it is important which team wins. So, we are stuck with all these interpretations.

Despite all the decisions of the international board and a variety of local rules by well-meaning administrators, there is still room for on-the-spot interpretation. Was the trip incidental? Was the handball accidental? Was the player in an offside position actually interfering with play? Was the ball completely over the line? Did the goalkeeper move before the penalty kick was taken? Usually! Is the defensive "wall" 10 yards away from the ball until a free kick is taken? Is a slide tackle or a jumping tackle dangerous? Sometimes! Was a shoulder charge too robust? Was a throw-in performed "correctly?" Did the offending player gain an advantage from his misconduct? Was the action malicious? Who was to blame – the high kicker or the low header? Is high kicking a crime? Was the shielding fair or an obstruction? Good referees make these judgment calls all the time and good players accept their decisions, even if they are wrong.

If a game lasts 90 minutes and there are 22 players, then on average each player has the ball for 90/22 = 3 or 4 minutes, or less, if you subtract the time that the ball is out of play or on its way from one player to the next.

If you look at the heart rates of good soccer players, you will see that they are two or three times their resting rate for most of the game, with occasional relaxation periods when the ball is out of play. Although your share of the ball maybe only two or three minutes, your job is to always be involved.

Chapter 23

Mathematical Permutations

Permutations are useful for determining alternate arrangements of players.

How many arrangements (permutations) can you make with 3 players standing in a line?

There are 3 ways of assigning the first player
2 of the second, 1 of the third
So the total number of arrangements is 3x2x1 = 6
3x2x1 is called 4 factorial and is written as 4!

In general, n factorial is written as n!.
n! = n x (n-1) x (n-2) x (n-3) x (n-4) . . . . x (1)

Consider the possible arrangements of players A, B, and C. There are six arrangements as illustrated in the chart below.

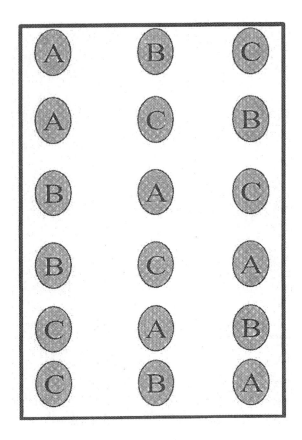

How many ways can you choose two players from a pool of four players? This is permutation of two items from four, which is calculated as shown below.

nPr = n!/(n-r)! = 4!/(4-2)! = (4)(3)(2)(1)/2! = 24/(2)(1) = 12

Some of the permutations are illustrated below.

Combination deals with a selection of so many items from a larger pool of items. Permutation deals with the arrangement of the selected items. So, in combination, A and B is the same as B and A. That is, one combination of two items. However, in permutation, A and B is a different arrangement from B and A. That is, two permutations of the two items. This distinction is important when arranging players in one order or another.

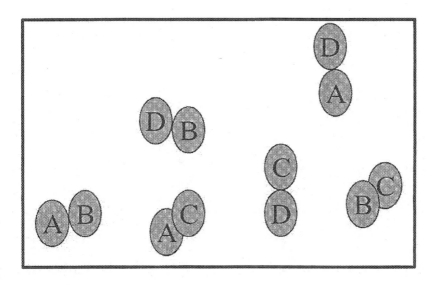

As another example, how many ways can you choose four players from 16? This is a combination question.

$$16!/4!(16-4)! = 16!/4!12! = (16)(15)(14)(13)/$$
$$(4)(3)(2)(1) = (4)(5)(7)(13) = 1,820$$

As you can see from the above example, a coach can have many, many, and many player line-up options. Of course, many of those options will be quickly invalidated due to infeasible matching of players. Nonetheless, the options are all there.

Chapter 24

Player Permutations and Combinations

A coach has a tremendous number of options in combination players to form specific team strength. Does player A play on the left of Player B or vice versa? Does Player A with skill X play in front of Player B with skill Y? These are some of the options that a coach has to be able to evaluate quickly. Knowing how to shuffle and reshuffle players is what makes many coaches great.

Permutations

A permutation is the choice of r things from a set of n things without replacement and where the order matters.

Suppose a coach wants to know in how many ways can eight players finish in a race (assuming there are no ties)? We can look at this problem as a decision consisting of 8 steps. The first step is the possibility of a player to finish first in the race, the second step is the player finishes second, . . ., the 8th step is the player finishes 8th in the race. Thus, by the Fundamental Principle of counting there are

$8 \cdot 7 \cdot 6 \cdot 5 \cdot 4 \cdot 3 \cdot 2 \cdot 1 = 40,320$ ways

This problem represents an example of an ordered arrangement. That is, the order that objects are arranged is important. Such an ordered arrangement is called a permutation. Products such as $8 \cdot 7 \cdot 6 \cdot 5 \cdot 4 \cdot 3 \cdot 2 \cdot 1$ can be written in a shorthand notation called factorial. That is, $8 \cdot 7 \cdot 6 \cdot 5 \cdot 4 \cdot 3 \cdot 2 \cdot 1 = 8!$, which is read as "8 factorial". In general, we define n factorial by

$n! = (n)(n - 1)(n - 2) \cdots 3 \cdot 2 \cdot 1$, if $n \geq 1$

If $n = 0$, we have $0! = 1$

Combination

A combination is the choice of r things from a set of n things without replacement and where order does not matter.

In a permutation, the order of the set of objects r people is taken into account. However, there are many problems in which we want to know the number of ways in which r objects can be selected from n distinct objects in an arbitrary order. For example, when selecting a two-player team from a club of 10 players, the order in the team is irrelevant. That is, putting Player A and Player B on a team is the same as putting Player B and Player A on the team.

- How many players on a team?
    - Any number, but in professional games there are 11 and about 5 substitutes, which added together makes 16.
    - This is a good number for a squad – it ensures that all players get a fair amount of playing time and leaves the team with enough players when some team members are not available to play.

- How many different kinds of practice game can you play with 16 players?
    - Any number – 8@1:1, 4@2:2, 2@4:4, 1@8:8.

- But what about 2:1, 3:1, 3:2, 4:3 and so on?
- *One strategic purpose of the game is for players to move about the field to create these numerical mismatches.*
- Now we have to find something to do with the remainders.
- • If you have 16 players at practice and play 2:1 games how many players are left out?

Arithmetic Groups and Combinations

- For the sake of convenience let us label our 16 players by the first 16 numbers or letters of the alphabet:
  - 1,2,3,4, 5,6,7,8, 9,10,11,12, 13,14,15,16
  - A,B,C,D, E,F,G,H, I,J,K,L, M,N,O,P

- Now let us divide the player into groups of 4 using the colors:
  - Red, Green, Blue and Yellow

- Now the players can keep the same number or letter for the season but they need not keep the same color for every practice. This way the coach can mix and match the stronger and weaker players.
  - If you really want to complicate things, you can assign different roles to each member of a group
    - • e.g., Left, Right, Forward, Back

- Think of how many different arrangements of 16 players can be made?

Fun with Poker Chips and Colored Bibs—Randomization

- Get 16 poker chips – 4 Red, 4 Green, 4 Blue, 4 Yellow – about 1 inch across (diameter)
- Shuffle the chips on the table and, with a ruler, arrange them in a straight line.
- With an erasable pen, mark them with the first 16 numbers or 16 letters of the alphabet.

– Divide them into groups of 4 by putting the same color together.
– Divide them into groups of 4, each group having 2 of one color and 2 of another
– Divide them into groups of 4, each group having 3 of one color and 1 of another.

- If you do this grouping with the player's labels face down, you have true randomization, but if you want to influence the group assignments then you can arrange them with the player number up.
- You can practice (pseudo)randomization on the practice field by
  – lining up the players and drawing out the colored bibs from a bag
  – having group (color) captains choose their teams
  – the coach assigning the colors
  – having players self select a color/team.

- Now you have an easy way of running the practice with groups of four

Allocating and Assessing Playing Time

- If a game lasts 60 minutes, how much playing time does each player expect to get?
  – It depends on how many players there are on a team. What if there are 11 players per team – making 20 over all, if we leave out the goalkeepers?
  – So, each player expects to have 60/20 = 3 minutes. Wow!
  – Now, if we assume that the ball is "in the air" or out of play for 30 minutes we are down to (60-30)/20 = 1.5 (that is 1 ½) minutes per player). Wow again!
  – Now if some players hog the ball and get twice as much of the action than the others, then these 10 ball hogs will get 2 minutes each and the other 10 will get 1 minute each. Wow!

- *So why are we tired after a game?*

   — *Because we do much more work – running – off the ball than with the ball.*

Using the Sets of Four

- If we practice for an hour in groups of 4, we will get much more ball time than if we practice in larger groups.
- If we stand in line waiting to run up and kick the ball under the eagle eye of the coach, the chances are we will get hardly any practice at all.
- By practicing in fours we can play all sorts of combinations – 4 together, 3:1, 2:2.
    - How many different game arrangements can you get using 4 players?
    - AvB, CvD, AvC, BvD, AvD, BvC – That's 6
    - A&BvC&D, A&CvB&D, A&DvB&C – That's 3
    - A&B&CvD, A&B&DvC, A&C&DvB, B&C&DvA – That's 4
    - A&B&C&D – That's 1
    - Or A,B,C,D on their own – That's 1
    - That makes a total of 15

Using combinations, permutations, and grouping, a system of player lineups can be developed. Below is one example.

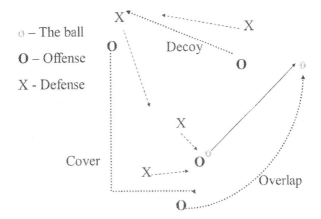

   o – The ball

   O – Offense

   X - Defense

Decoy

Cover

Overlap

Counting wins and losses

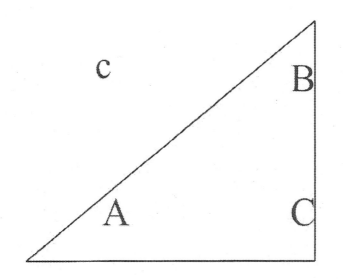

Chapter 25

Using Geometry for Player Lineups

The use of triangles plays an important role in soccer plays. Many practice sessions make use of three-person triangle formations to "knock" the soccer ball around. If used properly, you can throw opponents off their rockers by constantly shifting triangle patterns of ball movements. Triangulation, which is the process of measuring by using trigonometry, becomes second nature to top-notch players and it is used for keeping opponents running helter-skelter without effective contact with the ball. That is, an effective use of movement in time and space constitute playing field generalship that keeps opponents wondering what happened. Common triangle formations are illustrated below.

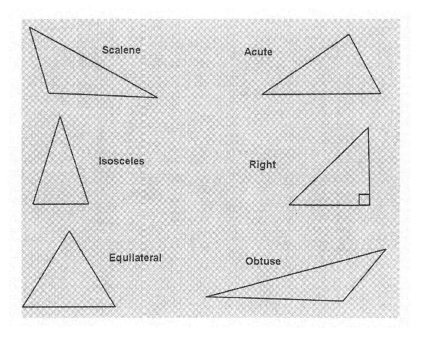

Scalene triangle

A scalene triangle with all sides of different lengths; no sides are equal and no angles are equal.

Acute triangle

An acute triangle is a triangle with its angles less than 90 degrees.

Isosceles triangle

An isosceles triangle is a triangle with (at least) two equal sides.

Equilateral triangle

An equilateral triangle is a triangle in which all three sides are equal. Equilateral triangles are also equiangular; that is, all three internal angles are also congruent to each other and are each equal to 60 degrees.

Obtuse triangle

An obtuse *triangle* is one where one of the internal angles is greater than 90 degrees.

Right triangle

A right triangle is a triangle with an angle of 90 degrees. The sides a, b, and c of such a triangle satisfy the Pythagorean theorem, which is represented as $a^2+b^2=c^2$, where the largest side is conventionally denoted c and is called the hypotenuse. The other two sides of lengths a and b are called legs. Self-initiated lone-practice sessions should be used to develop good soccer skills.

- How long is a line?
  - How far can you run, kick or throw?

- What direction does the line run?
- How many players make a triangle?
- How many triangles can you make with 4 players?
- What angle is between two lines?

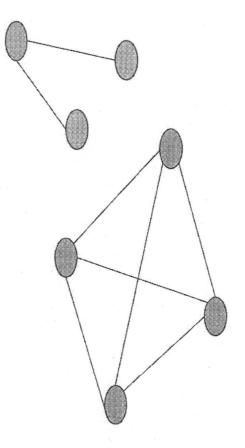

Passing and shooting targets

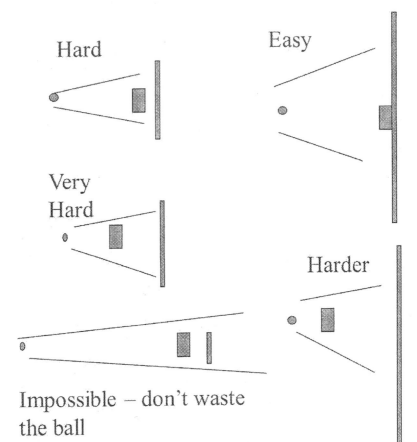

Hard

Easy

Very Hard

Harder

Impossible – don't waste the ball

The Bigger the Angle the Bigger the Target

Acute

The Bigger
the Angle the
Bigger the
Target

Obtuse

The closer
you are the
more
accurate the
pass or the
shot at the
goal

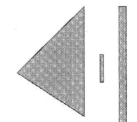

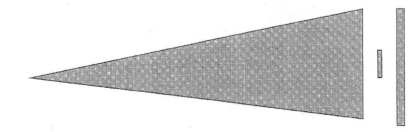

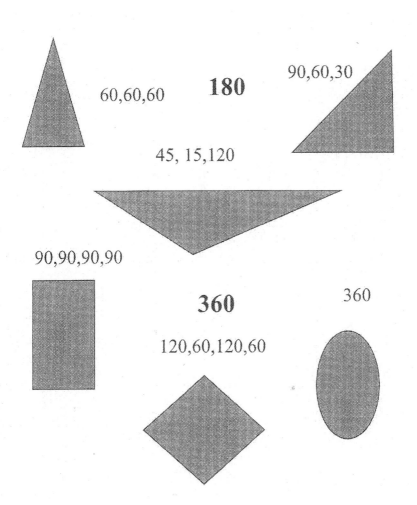

60,60,60   **180**   90,60,30

45, 15,120

90,90,90,90

360   360

120,60,120,60

Assessing Areas

- The area of a Rectangle is the length of adjacent sides multiplied together
- A Square is a rectangle in which all sides are equal
- The area of a Triangle is half the base times the height
- The area of a Circle is The Radius times the Radius times 22 divided by 7

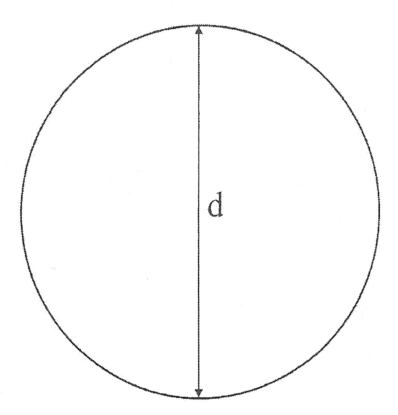

d = the diameter
r = the radius = half the diameter
c = the circumference = d*22/7
a = the area = r^2 * 22/7
   π (pi) = 22/7

If the center circle has a diameter of 20 yards what is its area?
If your thigh is 6 inches across, what is its cross sectional area?

What are the areas of the soccer field, the penalty area, the goal area, the center circle, the corner arc and the penalty restraining arc?

Pythagoras' Theorem

If you are standing on the edge of your penalty area in the middle of the field and your teammate is standing at the junction of the halfway line and the touch line, how far do you have to kick the ball?

What are a "square" and a "square root"?
The mathematics relationship of the sides of the triangle below is based on Pythagoras' Theorem, which is stated as follows

$$c^2 = a^2 + b^2$$

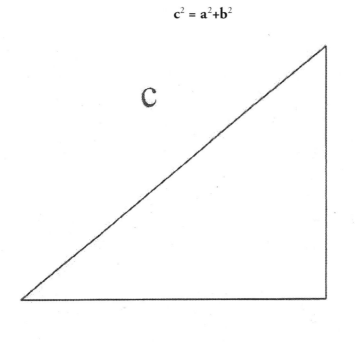

If you aim a corner kick at the penalty spot, what is the angle between your kick and the goal line?

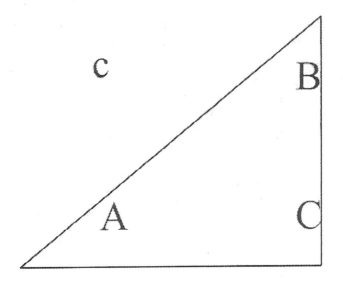

If Angle C = 90^0
sine (A) = a/c
cosine (A) = b/c
tangent (A) = a/b

If "a" is half the width of the goal and "b" is the shooter's distance from the goal, the chance of hitting the goal with a shot depends on the angle "A" – the effective target size.

- Sine Law (a / sin A = b / sin B = c / sin C)
- Cosine Law (c^2 = a^2 + b^2—2 a b cos C)

Vectors and Trajectories

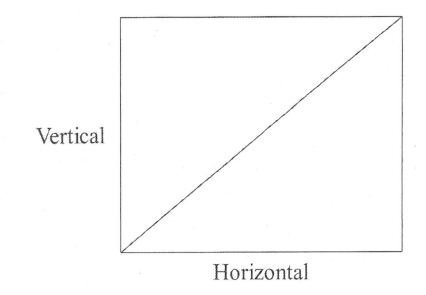

How far can you kick a ball?
How far can you throw a ball?
How far can you punt a ball?

- A vector is represented by a line segment
- Addition of vectors
- Resolution of vectors

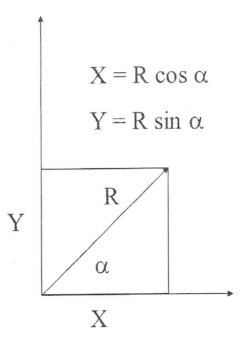

$$X = R \cos \alpha$$
$$Y = R \sin \alpha$$

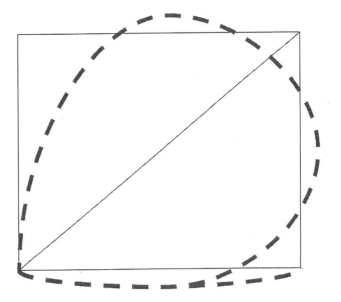

Chapter 26

Motion, Force, and Pressure

Motion Variables:

u = initial velocity
d = distance
t = time
a = acceleration
v = final velocity

Motion Equations:

$d = ut + \frac{1}{2} at^2$
$v^2 = u^2 + 2ad$
$v = u + at$

when u = 0, we have the following

$d = \frac{1}{2} at^2$
$v^2 = 2ad$
$v = at$

Motion Exercises
- Drop a heavy weight on your toe
  - What is the terminal velocity?

    – What is the kinetic energy?

    – What is the reaction force offered by your toe?

- Hit a golf ball with a 7 iron
  - How high will it go
  - How far will it travel forward

Impact of Forces

Recall Newton's Laws of Motion.
An object will remain stationary until acted on by a force.
How much acceleration can you give to the ball?
How far can you kick the ball?

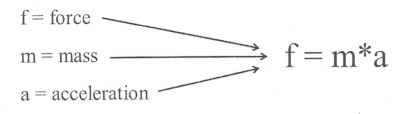

Implications of Newton's Laws

- I—A particle stays at rest or moves in a straight line at a constant velocity if there is no unbalanced force acting on it
- II—The acceleration of a particle is proportional to the resultant force acting on it and is in the direction of the force
- III—Action and reaction are equal and opposite

How high will a ball bounce?

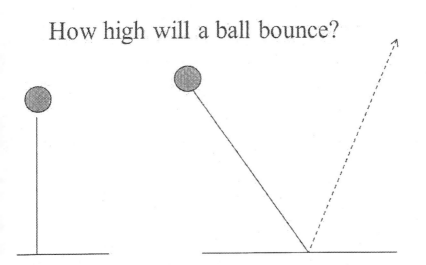

Pressure

How much air should we put into the ball?
What is the volume of the ball?
What is the inner surface are of the ball?

Consider pounds per square inch.

Pressure and volume are important.

Boyle's Law:

The pressure (p) of a given mass of gas, at constant temperature, is inversely proportional to its volume (v)

$p = 1 \, / \, v$

Boyle's law is an experimental gas law which describes how the pressure of a gas tends to decrease as the volume of a gas increases. A common statement of Boyle's law is

Deji Badiru

"The absolute pressure exerted by a given mass of an ideal gas is inversely proportional to the volume it occupies if the temperature and amount of gas remain unchanged within a closed system." The inside of a soccer ball is, indeed, a closed system. Mathematically, Boyle's law can be stated as

$$P \alpha \frac{1}{V}$$

Or

$$PV = k,$$

where P is the pressure of the gas, V is the volume of the gas, and k is a constant. The equation shows that, as volume increases, the pressure of the gas decreases in proportion. Similarly, as volume decreases, the pressure of the gas increases. For comparing the same substance under two different sets of condition, the law can be simply expressed as follows.

$$P_1 V_1 = P_2 V_2.$$

Chapter 27

Averages, Differences, and Ratios

On the average, if you play 10 games and score a total of 20 goals what is the average number of goals per game?

If two teams finish the season with the same number of points, the winner may be chosen by goal average or goal difference?

Team A scores 50 goals and gives away 25 goals

Goal average = 50/25 = 2

Goal difference = 50 − 25 = 25

Team B scores 20 goals and gives away 5 goals

Goal average = 20 / 5 = 4

Goal difference = 20 − 5 = 15

If we use averages the defensive team B wins, if we use difference the offensive team A wins. What should we do?

Probabilities

If we shoot 100 times from outside the penalty area we may score 10 times

The probability of scoring is 10/100 = 0.1

If we shoot 100 times from inside the penalty area we may score 50 times

The probability of scoring is 50/100 = 0.5

A "probability" is a number between 0 and 1 and it is the ratio of the number of successes to the number of attempts.

Chapter 28

Body Physiology: Heart, Lung, and Muscles

The Heart is the heart of the fitness needed to perform well in physical activities. Understanding heart rate in sports is essential for taking full advantage of the physiology of the body.

- Resting heart rate is between 50 and 80 beats per minute.
- When we run hard during a game it will increase to between 120 and 200 beats per minute.
- If we play a lot of sport our resting and exercise heart rates will go down because our hearts will get stronger and beat harder, thus pumping more blood per heartbeat.
- Some professional players have been clocked at an average of over 150 beats per minute over a whole game with some brief resting periods, when it drops to about 20 percent above the resting value.

The heart is often taken for granted because we don't see it. The risk of being out of sight and out of mind is the biggest danger of ignoring the heart in terms of the pressures and demands we put on it.

- The heart takes in blood through the right auricle, pushes it through the mitral valve to the right ventricle, then sends it to the lungs to take up oxygen and give off carbon dioxide before returning to the left auricle, through the tricuspid valve into the left ventricle and, from there, it circulates through the muscles, organs, brain and skin. Oxygenated muscles are required for movement.

The long and short of the lung is that it provides the avenue for staying alive through breathing.

- There is about 21 percent oxygen in the air we breathe in and about 16 percent in the air we breathe out.
- If we run hard and breath in and out 20 times a minute and use 4 liters of oxygen per minute, how much total air do we need to breath in on average in a single breath?

It is when we experience muscle aches and pains that we pay attention to our muscles.

- The strength of our muscles is related to the cross sectional area.
- If the diameter of our thigh is 8 inches and that of our upper arm is 4 inches and we can do a 50 pound curl how much could we lift by straightening our knee?

Chapter 29

Moments, Work, and Energy

- The further a weight is from the point of attachment of a muscle the harder it is to lift
- The quadriceps muscle attaches about 2 inches below the knee joint and the biceps (and brachialis) muscle attaches about 1 inch below the elbow, but the quadriceps has a cross sectional area that is four times that of the upper arm.
- If our forearm is is 12 inches long and our lower leg is 15 inches long what will be the ratio of the moments that we can exert with our arm and our leg.

Moment of Inertia

- Work = force x distance (Newton meters)
- Moment = force x displacement (Joule, Nm)
- Torque (moment)
- Energy—1 Joule = 1 Nm (Capacity for doing work)
- Potential Energy (position) weight * height
- Kinetic Energy (motion) m v^2 / 2

- Power = Force x velocity
            = Work / Time
  1 watt = 1 Joule / sec

- Momentum = mass x velocity
- Impulse = Force x Time
- Moment of Inertia = mass x distance squared

Useful Mechanical Units

- Scalars—Magnitude
  - e.g. mass, time, energy, speed

- Vectors—Magnitude and Direction
  - e.g. force, velocity

- Movement
  - Displacement (s)
  - Velocity (ds/dt)
  - Acceleration (ds/dt^2)
  - Jerk (ds/dt^3)

- Friction—Walking on ice
- Elasticity—A golf ball
- Compression—Joints
- Tension—Tendons and ligaments
- Shear—Intervertebral discs

Chapter 30

Statics and Dynamics

- Free body diagram (Force vector diagram)

  - Remove from surrounding structures
  - Resolve forces into components
  - Represent vectors by line length and direction
  - Draw the whole structure then separate diagrams

- Static Equilibrium
  - Sum of horizontal, vertical and rotational (moments) forces equals zero

Force (at a joint)= f(gravity, inertia)

- Inertia = mass x distance squared

- Swing a heavy and light hammer
- In cricket, big hitters use "the long handle", why?
- Figure skating
- Stopping an articulating arm with a heavy load

Chapter 31

Math and Science of Time Management

Why doesn't the best team always win?

Generally speaking the best team has the most shots at goal but the probability of a shot going in is very small and variable.

Say team A has 1000 shots on goal over the whole season and scores 50 goals in 25 games. That is averages of 40 shots per game, 1 goal for each 20 shots and 2 goals per game.

Team B has 750 shots and scores 75 goals in 25 games. That is averages of 30 shots per game, 1 goal for every 10 shots and 3 goals per game.

Given this information what is the probability (over time) that Team A will beat Team B, assuming they take 40 and 30 shots respectively?

Every activity takes time. Seconds count in everything.

How long does it take to . . . . do x, y, and z?

The most successful players manage their on-field time effectively by focusing on the techniques of the game. The reason many skilled players can fail on the field may have something to do with poor time management. Consider how long it might take to run from one end of the field to the other when play time is running out. Using field diagnostics through trigonometry, a player can pre-judge what is possible or not possible time-wise.

There are 168 hours in a week. Ideally your time should be divided equally between work, recreation and sleep . . . and practice time. This means:

- 56 hours work (things you have to do) per week
- 56 hours recreation (things you want to do) per week
- 56 hours sleep per week (8 hours per night)

This author has another guide book that introduces the "8 by 3 Paradigm of time management," in which each 24-hour day is divided into three blocks for work, home, and leisure activities. In a soccer game, the available playing time must be used efficiently and effectively to get the most out of each opportunity. The author's poem below emphasizes this point.

The Flight of Time (© 2006 Adedeji Badiru)
Time flies; but it has no wings.
Time goes fast; but it has no speed.
Where has time gone? But it has no destination.
Time goes here and there; but it has no direction.
Time has no embodiment; neither flies, walks, nor goes anywhere.
Yet, the passage of time is constant.

Chapter 32

Shapes on the Field

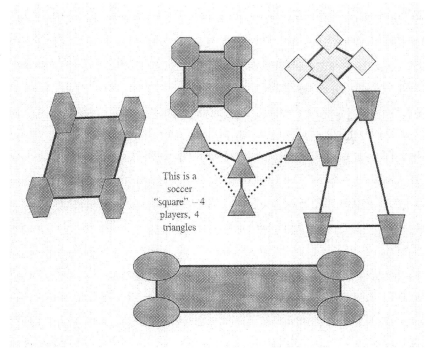

This is a soccer "square" — 4 players, 4 triangles

Four-sided figures don't always have equal length sides or right angles at the corners. It is no good having sides of the soccer figures that are too long or too short, otherwise, it either won't be possible to reach the other player with a pass or everybody will get too close and in each other's way. Players should learn to judge how far away they should be from the player with the ball.

How Many Triangles Can You Make by Connecting the Corners of a Four Sided Figure?

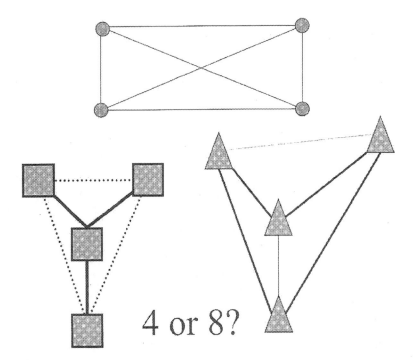

Chapter 33

Conclusion: Math Matters for Sports

As a concluding remark, "Youth Soccer Training Slides: A Math and Science Approach" confirms that math matters for sports, particularly soccer. The preceding chapters have presented concepts and examples of the application of science and math to the game of soccer. The purpose is not to present an in-depth theory of the applications, but rather to provide ideas to sensitize readers to the importance of analytical thinking in soccer and other sports.

Much has been said and written about the need to find new strategies to spark the interest of kids in STEM (Science, Technology, Engineering, and Mathematics) education, which is essential for preserving the nation's technological superiority and ensuring economic advancement. The key is to find the right "hook and bait" to get youngsters interested in technical and scientific fields. One hook that **Youth Soccer Training Slides** suggests is to use kids' interest in sports, particularly ball-based sports (soccer, basketball, tennis, softball, racquetball, etc.) to spark the interest of kids in embracing STEM fields. Recent studies have concluded that physical activities can enhance the learning potential of kids. Why not, then, channel that learning-physical-activity connection toward enhancing STEM education through a structured sports-and-STEM curriculum?

It has been recognized that future advancement of the nation will be dependent on STEM-oriented knowledge workers. The challenge of building the desired STEM-competent work force is to ensure that a sufficient number of students are entering STEM-related fields now. To this end, educational institutions are devising strategies to recruit, engage, and retain students in science and mathematics majors at the undergraduate levels. To make this happen, STEM educational opportunities and interests must be cultivated at middle to high school levels. The question is how to best ignite the interest of this class of students in science and mathematics early enough. postulates that such interest can be achieved if science education can be linked to something that most kids readily love to do. Sports! A specific example of this approach is the STEM-education-oriented website, www.physicsofsoccer.com, which presents an engaging connection between physics and soccer. Typical questions addressed by the website include the following.

- What makes a ball bounce?
- How gravity affects the flight path of a soccer ball?
- What makes a ball to bend in flight?
- How friction and moisture impede the game?

These are questions that inquiring little minds would be delighted to have answered in a fun relational way. For example, the flight path of a kicked soccer ball can be modeled to provide engaging simulation experiments to "wow" kids as they learn new concepts about gravity, lift, and drag without feeling intimidated. Cognitive awareness leads to pedagogical excellence.

With questions comes inquisitiveness. With inquisitiveness comes interest. With interest comes the self-actuated desire to learn more, which creates an opportunity to explain, engage, and retain attention for science and math principles. It has been shown that kids learn best when having fun. Using ball-based sports can open an avenue to explain the FUNdamentals of science to kids, whereby both boys and girls can equally benefit in the exposure to STEM without gender or socio-economic limitations.

It is the view of this author that every sports opportunity can be leveraged as a science and math learning opportunity. The key is to recognize and exploit the available opportunity. With this, STEM may very well spread more sustainably than we ever imagined.

Appendix A:

Distance conversion factors

Multiply	by	to obtain
angstrom	10^{-10}	meters
feet	0.30480	meters
	12	inches
inches	25.40	millimeters
	2.54	centimeters
	0.02540	meters
	0.08333	feet
kilometers	3280.8	feet
	0.6214	miles
	1094	yards
meters	39.370	inches
	3.2808	feet
	1.094	yards
miles	5280	feet
	1.6093	kilometers
	0.8694	nautical miles

millimeters	0.03937	inches
nautical miles	6076	feet
	1.852	kilometers
yards	0.9144	meters
	3	feet
	36	inches

1 Horsepower = 745.7 Watts
1 Atmosphere = 14.7 lb/in^2
1 BTU = 252 Calories (778 ft-lb; 1,054.8 Joules)
1 Radian = 57.3 degrees
1 Kilogram = 2.205 lb

Appendix B:

Tips and Guides for Ball Control

Heading the Ball

- Keep your eyes on the ball until it makes contact with your head.
- Estimate the height of the ball at the expected point of contact. Think geometry, trig., angles, and dimensions.
- Jump for the ball in a springy manner.
- Purposely hit the ball first . . . don't let it hit your head.
- Keep your neck muscles tightened.
- Make contact with the ball at your hairline.
- Outstretch your hands to brace your fall
- Soar for the ball and keep your head up to head the ball into the goal.
- Set up your body in anticipation of heading the ball.
- To go for the goal with an incoming high ball, instead of heading the ball, simply intercept its path using the surface area on your forehead slightly below the hairline.
- Just before the moment of making contact with the ball, turn your head in whatever direction you want the ball to go. This is how the greatest goals are scored with a header.

Receiving and Controlling the Ball

When you are in motion with the ball, it is more efficient to prepare the ball by redirecting it in a desired path rather than trapping it completely first, and then starting over. The fluid transition of the ball makes for a more effective action on the ball (Remember Newton's Laws of Motion).

1. Your target is to make contact with the middle or top part of the ball.
2. Softly tap the ball in the direction that you want to send it.
3. Practice receiving the ball away from the opponent. This gives you extra time by keeping you one step ahead of opponents and giving you more time for purposeful maneuvering of the ball.

Dribbling

- Dribble left and right (alternating) to keep opponents off balance.
- *Dance* with the ball. Make every move look good. Fluidity of motion not only impresses spectators, it also bamboozles opponents.
- Shield the ball away from opponents by controlling it on the far side of opponents
- Straddle the ball when in face-to-face close-contact dribbling situations. It allows better protection of the ball.
- Anticipate, execute collision avoidance, and avoid injury. Be mindful of Newton's second law of motion.
- Rein in the ball, put it under control, and maintain possession.
- Get the goalie on his knees with low shots toward the corner of the goal post.
- Scan the field and make *your* decision on the best person to pass the ball to. The loudest teammate calling for the ball is not necessarily the one with the best advantage.
- Look for openings through the formation of opposing players.
- Build speed and sprints to outpace opponents. Think of acceleration in Newton's Second Law of motion.

Ball Possession

- Be the center of attention when you have the ball in your possession. Do something with it. Capitalize on opportunities and maximize results. Game situation can change instantaneously.
- Don't just stand around. Be a part of the action. You are in play, even when you don't have the ball. Remember Newton's First Law of motion — A body at rest remains at rest until acted on by a force. That is, no motion, no action and no action, no motion.

Psyche Game

Sometimes, psychology works too. With the ball within your control, charge toward opponents and watch them retreat. It is a natural human reaction (at least for a quick moment) to retreat when charged at. By the time they recover their composure, you've done something meaningful with the ball. To do this, you must be able to make a fast decision during that brief instance that the opponents are befuddled. Nice trick or treat!

Shoulder-to-Shoulder

Build upper body strength to go shoulder-to-shoulder.
Conditioning, practice, proper diet, and endurance are essential for building strength for soccer excellence. Eating the right types of food at the right time helps to generate desired levels of energy. Strategic expenditure of the stored energy is essential for lasting through a grueling soccer match.

Chest Control

- Lean back and receive ball on your chest.
- Ball control has two main categories: **Receiving** and **Trapping.** Receiving is redirecting the ball to a spot useful for shooting or dribbling at the next touch while trapping is stopping the ball completely by cushioning it.

- Because of its broad surface and valley in the middle, the chest provides the largest surface area for trapping or receiving the ball. When using the chest for control, stretch out your arms and flex the muscles. When using the chest for ball cushioning, arch your back slightly. Depending on your starting stance, you may need to bend your knees or jump in order to align your chest with the height of the ball. Chest the ball up slightly to enable you to get your feet in the right position to take on the ball.

Practice makes Perfect

Practice to become a player of all parts
Use every legal part of the body to receive, trap, and control the ball.
Inside-of-the-foot ball control

1. Plant your supporting foot at about 45 to 90 degrees to the path of the ball.
2. Rest all of your weight on the foot and intercept the ball with the arch of your foot.
3. At the point of contact, cushion the ball by moving your foot toward the ball's original direction.
4. Instead of trapping the ball, you may wish to redirect it, whereby you simply turn your receiving foot in the desired direction.

Outside-of-the-foot ball control
This is useful when the ball is in motion ahead of you and moving from one side to the other.

1. Rather than turning your body into the ball's path, you can control it using outside of your foot.
2. Reach forward into the ball's path and intercept it with the outside of your foot. That will settle the ball because the outside of the foot provides a relatively large surface area.

Sole of the football control

1. Put your foot on the ball with your toes raised slightly above your heel.
2. Due to the faster pace of soccer nowadays, trapping with the sole of the foot is no longer used much to control passes.
3. Sole-of-the-foot control is, however, useful in dribbling. A player can use it to stop the ball before changing direction or in order to execute more intricate dribbling moves.

Thigh Ball Control

The thigh is especially effective for ball control.
Although you may not be able to redirect the ball with your thigh, you can cushion the ball with the thigh. This is efficient for receiving mid-air passes. A ball dropping (due to the effect of gravity) from a high pass can be received with the thigh. You must be able to adjust your stance or gait in order to position yourself to properly receive and control the ball.

1. Put your thigh in the path of the ball and retract as it touches you. If you don't retract properly, the ball may bounce off uncontrollably. Remember Newton's Third Law of motion — action and reaction of forces.
2. The segment of your thigh to use is above the knee up to about halfway of your thigh — certainly, not your knee, which, due to its hard surface, will result in a hard and uncontrolled bounce of the ball.
3. The inside of the thigh is good for stopping balls coming straight at you. In this case, open your lap and control the ball downward with the inside of your thigh toward your foot for a more deft control. You may use the outside of your thigh to direct the ball in the sideway direction that you will want to move after receiving the ball.

Always keep your eyes on high balls. Unexpected wind gust can wreak havoc on the anticipated path of the ball.

The demo on the left shows what can happen if you don't keep your eyes on the ball. You miss the ball and the ball misses you.

Instep Ball Control

This ball control technique is effective when the ball is falling toward you from a sharp angle.

1. As always, keep your eyes on the ball,.
2. Move quickly towards the ball's path so that you would not have to over-reach to control it.
3. Balance your weight on your supporting leg while you cushion the ball with your free leg.
4. Before the ball arrives, stretch the ankle of your free leg and relax the muscles of that leg. The ball should be controlled with the foot using the surface area around the shoelaces.
5. At the moment of contact retract your controlling leg by bending the knee and ankle—that will settle the ball down.
6. Take off with the ball using measured strides.
7. Pass off the ball while the going is good.

The Bicycle Kick

As beautiful as it is, performing a bicycle kick is risky and must be executed correctly. Only very skilled and well-practiced players should attempt it. Note the following:

- Brace yourself with your arms as you land back on the ground.
- The difficulty of the move makes it unanticipated and, therefore, has potential for injury.

Tips and Guides:

1. Keep **your back** to the target and your eyes on the ball. Target is most often the goal.

2. Bring the knee of your non-kicking leg toward your chest followed immediately with the same motion of your kicking leg. The movement of your legs will appear as if you're pedaling a bicycle backwards. Hence, the name of the maneuver.
3. Extend your kicking leg to meet the ball while you are airborne and falling backwards.
4. Pedaling down with your non-kicking leg, kick through the ball.
5. Pull your toes back so your ankle makes a right angle as you connect with the ball.
6. Extend both arms and your palms facing the ground behind you to brace yourself.
7. Watch the knee of your kicking leg until you are on the ground to insure that you don't land head first.

No diving zone !

There should be no feet-first diving at the ball when it is clearly rolling out of bounds. What is the point? Gusto? Hustle commendation? Show off? Hoopla? Contesting for goalie job?
There is no point.
Except to risk injury and make yourself look silly.

Triangles

Triangles win games
Triangulation of play keeps opponents guessing and off balance.

Joy of the Game

Celebrate goals with teammates. It builds team spirit. Have fun with the game.

About the author

Deji Badiru is an award-winning author, educator, researcher, and administrator. He is a registered professional engineer, a Fellow of the Institute of Industrial Engineers, and a Fellow of the Nigerian Academy of Engineering. He holds a B.S. in industrial engineering, an M.S. in mathematics, an M.S. in industrial engineering from Tennessee Technological University, and a Ph.D. in industrial engineering from the University of Central Florida. Badiru also holds a leadership certificate from the University of Tennessee. He is a member of several professional organizations and author of several books and technical journal articles. He has served as a consultant to several organizations around the world and has received awards for his teaching, writing, and leading teams. Badiru has diverse areas of avocation. His professional accomplishments are coupled with his passion of writing about everyday events, interpersonal issues, and social observations.